Beautifully BROKEN

How God Healed *My Broken, Shattered Heart* and Brought Forth A Lioness

DEBORAH BLAKEY

BEAUTIFULLY BROKEN: How God Healed My Broken,
Shattered Heart and Brought Forth A Lioness

By Deborah Blakey

©2022 by Deborah Blakey

ISBN#979-8-9868110-0-0

Author: Deborah Blakey
Editor: Valerie L. McDowell
Cover Design: danny_media
Interior Book Design: Velin@Perseus-Design.com
Publisher: Power2Excel Agency, LLC

Scripture taken from The Bible: Authorized King James
Version (KJV). Oxford: Oxford University Press.

Also used, The Holy Bible: New international version, containing the Old Testament
and the New Testament. (1978). Grand Rapids: Zondervan Bible Publishers.

Also used, The Holy Bible: The Amplified Bible. 1987. 2015.
La Habra, CA: The Lockman Foundation.

Printed in the United States of America.

What Others Are Saying ...

My journey with Deborah started with me ministering to her as I witnessed her struggles turn into victories. We became very close, and her trust in me grew. Then the tables turned, and she became my life coach. During our sessions, she helped me see areas of my life that needed mending, places where I needed to step up and stop allowing people to hurt me.

Deborah taught me to love myself and look to God for validation, not man. She taught me to protect my heart and be strong and reminded me of what God said about me and how what he says about me is all that matters. Not only was she teaching me, but she modeled it for me every step of the way. I grew much in my walk and life with Deborah as my coach. I am forever grateful to God for bringing this amazing lady into my life.

Elder Robin Ferguson,
Faith and Family Church

Deborah Blakey is a spiritual woman of God whose actions represent her belief in Jesus. Her faith reflects her love for people and shows up in her everyday walk. She represents the hands and feet of Jesus in her personal life and my experience with her as a leader. I am proud to have her on my team as a leader but even more blessed to know her as a person and a friend."

Matt Martinez,
District Office, Richmond/Tidewater, VA

I first met Deborah around 2010. I always saw her as a kind and beautiful woman...always smiling and willing to help wherever possible. However, a few years ago, I worked with Deborah when she started her coaching business...Beautifully Broken! Just the name of her business spoke volumes to my heart. I was heartbroken when she worked with me due to an event over 20 years ago. I struggled so much and did not know how to handle the pain of it. With Deborah's coaching, encouragement, and sharing of her testimony, she helped me to move forward with my healing process.

Deborah continues to be a positive presence in my life and is always there to listen and share godly wisdom and direction. She still has that beautiful smile and servant's heart...I still reach out to her for guidance and direction. Deborah is an excellent example of a Proverbs 31 Woman of God!

Erica D. Lee,
Manager, Data Analytics for Gov't Programs, Synterra Health

The day I met Deborah, I knew it would be a lifetime connection. We connected while attending a retreat at the Health Coach Institute in Phoenix, AZ, and shortly after that as roommates for a Master Transformation Coaches retreat in San Diego, CA. I learned so much about Deborah, including the actual pronunciation of her name. She explained that many people called her "Debra," but her name was Deborah, just like in the bible. Deborah, the prophetess who was the only female judge, was deeply concerned over the ill-treatment the Israelites suffered at the hands of their Canaanite enemies. And just like the Deborah in the bible, the Deborah I met was wise and carried much faith in her heart, believing that God would use her to help heal the broken-hearted. Deborah uses her pain as power as she walks out her calling: to advocate for those who need guidance, pray for those who feel hopeless, and help set captives free from the true enemy, the devil. I'm thankful to God for putting Deborah in my life. She has been supportive of me and my ministry from day one. Thank you, Momma Deborah; you are truly a blessing to many. I love you.

Dana Watson, M. Ed., M.A., C.HC
Owner & Master Transformation Healing Coach, Elev8te
Health & Wellness, LLC

Deborah Blakey is a phenomenal Woman of God with whom I've had the privilege and honor of fellowshipping and frequently worshipping over the past seven years. From the moment I met her, I knew she loved and served God wholeheartedly and loved everyone unconditionally. Her life's work has always been focused on the spiritual well-being of others. She truly believes in total wellness; physical, mental, emotional, and financial. Her commitment to improving everyone's life is sure to come through in this her first literary work. If she is half the author that she is an entrepreneur, fitness enthusiast, and passionate worshipper, then this book will completely change numerous lives. Get ready to be moved emotionally, inspired intellectually, and enlightened spiritually as you read this anointed book by my blessed sister Deborah Blakey.

Pastor Rodney W. Gilchrist, Founder/Senior Pastor
Liberty Christian Center, Killeen, Texas

We met Deborah Blakey nine years ago when she came into our ministry. She entered our church with a sweet, warm, and compassionate spirit. We quickly learned what a fun-loving woman of God she is. Deborah continues her walk with Jesus Christ, despite the obstacles and challenges she has faced. She allows nothing nor anyone to stop the calling that God has on her life. Deborah encourages women to know and love Jesus Christ through the word of God. She empowers and uplifts others to reach heights beyond their original goal or vision. She breeds confidence as an entrepreneur and a fitness guru who takes care of her mind, body, and soul, showing others that "you matter." As she is biblically grounded, she can relate and communicate with believers and non-believers. She is a leader among leaders! We are better because of her.

Pastors/Founder Calvin and Barbara Duncan
Faith and Family Church, Richmond, VA

Dedication

First and foremost, I am thankful to God, my Father, who never allowed me to give up on myself. Everything I am is because of His love for me.

Second, I dedicate this book to the heavy-hearted, those who have experienced and endured...

Abuse
Abandonment
Depression
Low Self-Esteem, and
Rejection.

Finally, I write this book absolutely convinced that God can take all the broken pieces of your heart and thoughts and make something beautiful.

I pray that you find healing, love, peace, and your life's value in these pages. I also pray it provokes you to live the life you were intended to live as you read through my journey to becoming the greatest version of who I know I was meant to be.

With all my love,
Deborah

For I am convinced that neither death nor life, neither angels nor demons, neither the present nor the future, nor any powers, neither height nor depth, nor anything else in all creation, will be able to separate us from the love of God that is in Christ Jesus our Lord.

~ROMANS 8:38-39

Acknowledgments

To my Mother, thank you for showing me so much love for the short time I had you on this earth. My goal has always been to be the type of woman you could be proud of. Making you proud has been my driving force in life for so long. Even when I wanted to give up, I couldn't because, in my mind, if I could live after you died, I could live through anything. I look forward to seeing you again.

"My mother was my role model before I knew what that word was."
~LISA LESLIE

To my Grandmother, thank you for all the sacrifices you made for my siblings and me, but most importantly, my mother. You taught me to never give up on God and always to trust God in everything. Because of your love for God and ensuring that my siblings and I stayed in church every Sunday, I could find my way back to God. I will always be grateful for that and the unconditional love you showed.

To my children: James, Irene, and Isiah, you are my heartbeat. I am thankful God chose me to be your mother. I am so blessed to experience your unconditional love and support for everything I do. Because of my love for you, I am saved and live the life that God intended for me to live. You are God's gift to me.

Behold, children are a heritage from the LORD; The fruit of the womb is a reward.

~Psalms 127:3

To my Grandchildren, who inspire me to always reach for the stars. I am so happy to have you in my life. You are a gift I could've never imagined. When I see you, not only do you light up the room, but you also light up my heart. I want to teach you through my life that it isn't always going to be easy, but you can be, do, and have everything your heart desires if you never give up. You are my Legacy!

To my Siblings: God, what can I say? No matter the trial, obstacle, trauma, or even drama, whether side-by-side or miles apart, we have made our parents proud by always having each other's back. We have been through hell and high water, but one thing is for sure, we have loved each other unconditionally through it all! As Carl Dean (Dad) used to tell us all the time, and I quote, "We all we got!" The love I have for you all is unexplainable.

Contents

Foreword

I have known Deborah for nearly thirty years as a pastor, counselor, and friend. My heart is deeply touched as I hear much of her story for the first time!

Beautifully Broken reminds us that we all have stories we have never allowed others or even ourselves to hear. When we finally embrace the script of this movie we call our lives, we discover that there is more beauty than brokenness.

As you read Deborah's story, think about your own story. Have you suppressed some of the "ugly" chapters and, in so doing, missed the beauty that lies beneath?

This book will give you peace about your past, strength for the present, and faith for an amazing future.

B. Courtney McBath, Senior Founding Pastor
Calvary Revival Church, Norfolk, Virginia

Introduction

In 2007, after five years of marriage, I was numb. Things had gotten so bad that my own children didn't want to live with my husband and me anymore. They went to live with their father because my home had become a ticking time bomb.

I had to do something. This life was not what I planned for, hoped for, or even prayed for. I knew I needed to get away. So I went to my happy place, my safe place, the place I go to talk with God. I went to the beach. You know water has such a calming and soothing effect on so many people. I love being at or by the water. So off I went. It wasn't that far away, and I went there to get some solace. To get some peace from all the trauma I was experiencing in this marriage that I thought was from God.

After I drove to the beach and parked, I got out and started walking in the sand toward the water. I was looking ahead and walking into the ocean. All I can remember after that is my girlfriend grabbing me and pulling me back. I don't remember how she got there or even knew where I was. And I don't remember thinking I wanted to die. But I also don't know how to swim. Yet I was walking straight into the water. It had gotten about waist high when I felt these hands grabbing me and holding me tight, calmly saying, "Let's go."

Once we got back, she never brought it up. She never talked about it to me. She never asked me why I was trying to kill myself or even if that was what I was doing. She was just there for me.

But I knew God must have told her where I was because I never did. I didn't call a soul or tell anyone what I was going through in my marriage. Looking back, that was the only time in my life that I knew that I felt suicidal. And it was also at that moment that I realized how much God loved me and that he would send help to rescue me.

He will do the same for you.

But let me go back. Let me go back to the beginning so you can understand how I got to this point.

Chapter 1

It Wasn't Supposed To Turn Out This Way (Broken and Scared)

> Our deepest fear is not that we are inadequate. Our deepest fear is that we are powerful beyond measure. It is our Light, not our Darkness, that most frightens us.
>
> ~MARIANNE WILLIAMSON

I grew up in Filbert, Pennsylvania, a small country town in Fayette County that barely gets a dot on a map. It lies between Morgantown and Pittsburgh, so that you can make your way here from West Virginia or Maryland. People usually call our town Republic or Fayette County when any mention of how to get here arises because to say Filbert means nothing if you're not from 'round here. But we were. We were raised with my mother and grandmother in a two-bedroom home. We lived in several places; some were farms, and some were just a lot of land in the middle of nowhere.

My mom had four girls and then four boys. I'm the oldest, and there are ten years between my youngest sibling and me. I was the oldest but very shy, so please don't ask me to talk in front of people. Not my thing. Having the other kids do their thing was a blessing because it shielded me from being front and center. I figured I had my moment to be doted on as the firstborn, but since we are all stair-step children, my time in the limelight was short-lived.

There was always lots of noise around, including doors slamming, kids running, and all kinds of food, clothes, books, or toys lying everywhere. But that was normal. Having a spotlessly clean house all the time was just a fantasy in a house of eight children. And it helped that we lived out in the country. We had plenty of space to roam around and play outside, making good ground for a child's imagination. Now for those that know, just a few miles outside of any major city can seem like a whole other world, and back in the 60s, and 70's, when my siblings and I grew up, our world was very country. But we had the best mother. She was wonderful. She indulged in our constant talking, bickering, and play fighting until she reached her breaking point. Then all she had to do was give us a look, and we all settled down immediately! But she also was hardworking like most women then and now.

My mother was also a powerful black woman that did not play. That meant it better be done if she left the house for work with clear instructions on what we were to do while she was gone. And even if she came home at 2:00 am and something was not done that she told us to do before she left, she'd wake us up out of our sleep and make us do it. And the wake-up call was usually with a belt or a switch. So it didn't take too many of those reminders for us to be able to sleep through the night peacefully, knowing nothing was left undone.

Most of Mom's time was spent working to keep a roof over our heads and clothes and food on our backs and bellies. Therefore, occasionally ignoring us was probably more of a science she had perfected. She usually rested her eyes between jobs knowing that our chores were done and homework was completed and correct. She didn't tolerate anything less, and we knew it. She was wonderful but strict. And she didn't stand for rebellious kids. We knew what she expected, and we knew the limits. Besides, with eight kids, even she knew it wouldn't be quiet most of the time unless we were sleeping.

My fondest memories with my mom were from when we were young girls. My sisters and I all had long hair, and we kept to ourselves, mainly because we had each other to entertain. Also because my mom made us all stick together. She told us that if she caught somebody messing with one, they better know they were messing with us all, and we better take up for them right there. And it seemed we had to use it directly after she told us that.

One day we were getting off the bus, and our neighbors came over and started messing with us. I'll never forget them. Their last name was Hall, and they called us "nappy heads" and would chase us off the bus all the way home. We'd be running, trying to get away from them, but they would catch us and start pulling our hair or trying to hit us.

My mom was home and happened to be looking out the window when we were getting chased home from the bus. When we got to the front door, she opened it and said, "What are you doing?" She told us to go back down the street and said, "if you don't kick their ass when you come back here, I'll send you outside to get a switch, and I'll do it for them." She was like, beat them or get beat. So not wanting to feel her wrath, we went back out there and beat them up good. After that day, they never chased us again. My mom was teaching us to stand up for ourselves. She would not allow us to run from anything. She also made sure we stayed little girls as long as possible. I had a lot of white friends in our community, and many wore makeup and skimpy clothes at 11 and 12 years old. We were not allowed to do any of that. Even when it came to our hair, and we had a lot of it, it had to be braided or in some ponytail. We were kids and raised as such.

Now no matter how many hours my mother worked, there was one thing we could always count on: going to church. When the doors opened up Sunday morning, we were all going to be there, nice and shined up in our Sunday best. And it was our grandmother who kept us in church. This was the balance to the tough love we experienced from our mother. However, Grandma would always tell us, "Do not talk to boys," and "Don't do nothing with no boys, nothing at all until you're married or you're going to hell."

My grandmother didn't play either, but she was more loving toward us because she knew we would be lost without her attention, care, and affection. My grandmother gave my mother her last name, which was Blakey. It was years later that I learned this information. One day I came across her birth certificate after going through some of my mom's things. The birth certificate said Irene Dawson was the mother. The woman we knew as our grandmother wasn't my mother's mother. She was her great-aunt, her grandmother's sister. My mother was left on the doorstep for her aunt to raise. She had no children of her own and raised my mother as her daughter.

My mother did not have quality relationships with the men in her life. Two of my sisters and I had one father, whom I cannot remember ever meeting or knowing as a child. However, I found out later that he lived close enough to see us growing up without ever contributing to our physical or emotional needs. My baby sister and four brothers had a different father, Carl Dean, who was around but barely. So the only father we knew was my sister's and brothers' father, and Mom made us call him Dad. But like I said, he was in and out of our lives a lot, mostly out.

However, I do remember some good times with Carl Dean. At Christmas, he would dress up as Santa Claus and come to the house. He would be full of energy and laughter, telling jokes and trying to make us laugh. With all his children, we usually only got one gift, but it didn't matter; we were all right. We were happy kids. We didn't want for anything. We always had plenty of food on the table, and although we did not have what people might have considered the best things, that wasn't important. We had our mom and our grandmother, who took us to church to learn about Jesus. So we didn't know what we didn't know. But we knew Mom made us love each other and protect each other. The closeness of the family meant everything to her and us.

Unfortunately, the good times with Dad did not happen consistently. He was often drunk and violent. It was nothing for him to drag my mother out of the house and beat her, really bad, with us and the whole neighborhood secretly watching out of the bedroom window - us ashamed and the neighbors in shock. After he was done and passed out, I was the one that would come out of my room, helping my mom inside and cleaning her up. I always took care of her. My mother wouldn't call the police. What she would say to me as I wiped away blood or helped her change her clothes confused me. She said, "Don't blame him. What happens between us is none of your business."

I'm pretty sure this was when my anxiety started. None of my business??? It was the whole neighborhood's business, as we all knew. So, of course, I said nothing back to her, and I certainly didn't tell my siblings, though they saw and heard everything, too, as did everyone else within earshot. But in our house, it all stayed hush-hush. We have never talked about him beating our mother to this day. My siblings and I have never talked about how we grew up in this environment with each other.

Yet even though we did not talk about it, my grandmother did. She hated my dad. I secretly did too. What kind of man does this? And why did she always take him back? My disillusionment with their relationship and growing hatred of him intensified once I realized I had seven other brothers and sisters.

I'm not sure what family he stayed with; I only know he didn't stay with my mom and us a lot. But sometimes, out of the blue, he would show up at our house while mother was at work and make all of us go with him, piling us into his car.

Dad had a huge car; it could've been a "deuce and a quarter," as they called it back then. Whatever it was, it could fit all of us kids in there. Then off we'd go to some other woman's house. This happened many times over the years with many different women.

My mom had just gotten off work the first time this happened and found the house empty. She freaked out. Knowing how badly he treated her, her first thought was that he had done something to us.

She searched for us in all the places she knew he frequented, including his family's home. She was devastated by his behavior. But after searching multiple locations and finally found us, she would gather us all up to take us back home.

These behaviors infuriated my grandmother. Her hatred towards him only increased. Yet Mom would say nothing against him; Carl Dean was whom she loved. I don't know what she saw in him, especially when he had much more going on than my mother.

This crazy relationship went on my whole childhood. The same thing repeatedly happened, with him disappearing for weeks or months at a time, then suddenly showing back up. He was the only man I ever saw with my mother.

My Heroes

Strength, Courage, and Unconditional Love
From Youngest to Oldest: Paul Blakey, Leslie Blakey, Carl (Rooten)
Blakey, Andre Dean (Ko), Crystal Blakey, Amelia Dean (Vern),
Sylvia Blakey (Syl the Bill), Dorothy Blakey (Doris), Deborah
Blakey, Montean Dean (Tangi) and Carl Dean, Jr. (Bug)

***

I'll never forget one night when my mother came home from work. She was exhausted and complained of having a horrible headache. "I want to lay down. I want to rest," she said. She looked awful, to the point that my sisters and I, even Granny, said, "Maybe you should go to the emergency room." Then, finally, she said, "No, I'll go tomorrow. Let me lie down."

Granny started dinner and fed everyone, and I checked on my siblings' homework. Then, I made sure the house was clean. Mom was still lying down in her room downstairs as we all got ready for bed. We figured she must have been exhausted, so I went upstairs to bed after ensuring everything was in place.

Late into the evening, we heard this big thump. My grandmother called out to me but yelled, "Deborah." I almost didn't remember my name because everybody called me Debbie. No one used Deborah much, and only my mom if she was mad at me. Then I heard my grandmother scream my name, telling me to come downstairs. I sat on the step for a while because, in my heart, I knew what had happened. I couldn't go down the stairs. I couldn't move. I just sat there staring until her screams pierced my soul. I jumped up and ran down the stairs. My mom was on the floor.

Mom died on March 24, 1972. I had just turned 13 years old the month before. This was not how I thought my teen years would begin. Everything was at warp speed after that. The shock, the tears, the funeral. Everything was a blur to me. My sister told me I tried to climb into the casket. I have no recollection of that.

But I remember that this was also the day my grandmother's spirit left her body. She was in the house, but mentally and emotionally, she was gone. She was little more than a shell of a person after Mom died. The loss did something to her from which she never recovered. Grandma became sick soon after Mom died, which started her decline.

Granny told me that since I was the oldest, I had to step up and help her. So that's what I did. I jumped right in and took up the slack. I was 13, and my little brother was three. So what I needed didn't matter as long as my seven brothers and sisters got what they needed.

With mom gone, life moved quickly. At thirteen, I went from this shy girl to head of household and leader of the family. I assumed the role of mom, dad, teacher, leader, anything and everything I needed to be. I never thought about my age, the unfairness of life, or whatever you're supposed to feel when something tragic like this happens. I just did what needed to be done. I did what my mom and grandmother needed me to do to keep our family together.

And I was ok with that. My siblings' well-being was my motivation. I just wanted to make Mom proud. I needed my mom to be proud of me. I didn't think about myself anymore. I wasn't even concerned about my grades, but I ensured all my sisters and brothers kept up with their studies. Even when I entered high school, many of the activities and friendships that were normal I didn't have. I never went to prom or school dances, or other events. I had to take care of my family.

I believe a mental shift had occurred in my mind, saying, this is my life. I also know it was God who strengthened me for this role. But then, I blamed God for taking away the one person who loved us on this earth. And even though I knew my grandmother loved us, it didn't make up for losing our mother.

However, just because I did not deal with my emotions concerning my mother's death didn't mean they didn't exist. I just pushed them aside like I did everything else in that season. The busyness of everything I was doing kept my mind off how I felt for years. Yet I couldn't shake the anxiety that was growing around my heart. I was internally on edge and always wondering what else would happen. I tried to figure out why I was so anxious, but I didn't know how to fix it, so I tucked it all away.

My First Love

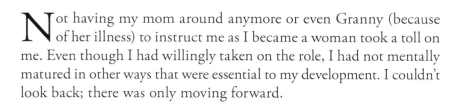

A woman is like a tea bag; you never know how strong it is until it's in hot water.

~Eleanor Roosevelt

Not having my mom around anymore or even Granny (because of her illness) to instruct me as I became a woman took a toll on me. Even though I had willingly taken on the role, I had not mentally matured in other ways that were essential to my development. I couldn't look back; there was only moving forward.

When I turned 14, I was old enough to get a job. Now, besides cooking, cleaning, and taking care of my siblings and Granny at home, I started working at Fishers' Big Wheel to help financially. Fishers' Big Wheel, sometimes known as just Fishers', was a discount department store chain based in New Castle, Pennsylvania. It was a pretty big chain of stores in our area when we were growing up. I worked there for three years. Unfortunately, they closed down in the early 1990s.

Ever since mom died, Granny was not well. She went from just being heartbroken to multiple kinds of illnesses. I'm pretty sure she had Alzheimer's or dementia. But back then, you heard little about that disease, but the signs were all there compared to now. I remember times when we played, laughed, and talked, and Granny suddenly thought we were talking about her. She also started fussing more than usual and repeatedly asking us the same questions or telling the same story.

Then there might have been something wrong with her kidneys because I vaguely remember her wearing a colostomy bag on her stomach because her bladder or intestines were not working correctly. It was sad watching Granny getting sicker and sicker. Then her health declined to where doctors did not give her long to live. Granny succumbed to her various illnesses and died on January 12, 1975, three years after Mom.

My brothers and sisters and I were now orphans. We didn't have any other family because Carl Dean was not in the picture. And as I try to figure out what to do, I'm still figuring out that every-day matters as well. So I reached out to my sister Tedda for help. So Tedda and her husband Dave, who had recently married, moved in with us in that two-bedroom rented house. Now there were 10 of us in the small place. They got one of the bedrooms, and the rest of us did as we always did, slept wherever we could, pallets on the floor, the couch, and in the other bedroom. We stayed in that house for about a year and a half.

Now you can imagine that with that many of us living together, basically kids and teenagers with no real steady income, we often lacked the necessities. There were times we did not have running water, and the house was in pretty bad shape and needed a lot of repairs. At some point, our dad, Carl Dean, stayed there for a while. I cannot fathom why but I also don't remember him being there at all, probably because so much was happening at once. My brother told me he thinks I don't remember this period the way he does because my mindset was all about taking care of everybody and everything. Perhaps I was just traumatized. He thinks I was. We all were. But more so me because I assumed responsibility for everyone.

Life moved on.

Throughout the loss of my mother and grandmother and through all the upheavals in trying to keep a roof over our heads, I had a good friend named Lucy, who had been watching my life break down before her eyes. Lucy was very outgoing and confident, whereas I was timid. Lucy took me under her wing and did her best to help me get my mind off everything constantly swirling around me. And Lucy was determined to get me to start having some fun while I was still a teenager.

Her first goal was to set me up with a boy. Looking back, I know God put her in my life because she helped me overcome my shyness. I was so nervous that I couldn't even talk to people without feeling so embarrassed that I usually ran away. But like I said, Lucy was determined to make a real teenager out of me.

The first guy she set me up with, she groomed him first, telling him I was "different" and to be ready for me. She invited me to her house and told me this guy was on his way. But before he got there, she had already told him, "Listen, under no circumstances do you try to kiss her. I'm serious. Don't do that at all." So anyway, she left us downstairs while she went upstairs. We talked for a little while, but then he leaned over to kiss me, and all I could do was scream. It was crazy. I was 14 years old, but I was screaming for my friend to come and save me because this guy was trying to kiss me. I was screaming y'all. This is how shy I was. I'm screaming, and Lucy comes running downstairs and cusses him out, then puts him out. He was shocked, but I smiled, thinking, "that's a good friend." She was like, "I told you not to touch her." But I was OK with it, like I said. I think Granny had so ingrained in me, and us girls, that we were going straight to hell if a boy so much as touched us. (Anyway, although Lucy and I don't talk anymore, she is forever in my heart, and I will always love and appreciate her friendship.)

Now keep in mind that because of how we were raised, there had never been any discussions about normal boy-girl feelings with

Granny or my mother. Nothing about anatomy, how this is normal, what to look out for, or even expect. They didn't even say anything about sex not being a good thing, or you might get pregnant. Nope. None of that. You only heard the fear of God and going to hell if a boy so much as touched you. And in that instance, my shyness and inexperience worked well for me. He never came back, and I could be my regular self again. I was good with that because I just wanted to stay in my comfort zone. My comfort zone was taking care of my family. My comfort zone was making my momma proud. And again, the only thing that stayed on my mind was all I had to do now that Granny was also gone.

As life progressed and we all got older, to Lucy's delight, I started seeing a guy named James, whom we all called Fats. He was a few years ahead of me in school, and a football player, which meant all the young ladies tried to get with him. But he was cool and never tried to force me to do anything, not that I was going to anyway, although he tried things like any regular guy would. My friends couldn't believe I could tell him, "I don't want to do this," and he wouldn't try to force me. He respected me even though everybody else was doing their thing. But as I said, I was ok with it because my mom didn't allow us to wear makeup and none of that, and he liked me as I was. She raised us strictly to be church girls.

How our mom and Granny raised us, however, laughed at by many, also made us unique and, for many guys, desirable. Also, remember, back in those days, we didn't have cell phones, the internet, or any quick ways of reaching people. If they weren't home, you left a message with whoever answered the phone, hoping they wouldn't forget, and waited for them to call you back. And if someone lived in another state, you had to make a long-distance call or call someone collect or reverse the charges from your phone. You had to pay extra for any calls that were not local. And, of course, no one had any money for that. So just keeping in touch was a big deal, but being the oldest and in charge gave me a lot more leeway to talk with Fats.

Anyway, we went out for a couple of years. As he headed toward high school graduation, there was talk about people going to college, and everyone knew he was headed there. So Lucy and some other girls started talking about how I needed to give my man some before he went to college and hooked up with the women there on campus. Being shy, I was never one to give in to peer pressure. Plus, I had missed so much of the normal transitions teens went through during high school while raising my brothers and sisters that it was never a thing for me. As I contemplated his leaving and my next move, I gave in and gave it up. And it hurt. And I got pregnant. ON THE FIRST TRY!!!! Really. After hearing my mom and Granny's constant mantra in my head about not letting boys even touch you until you're married, now here I was, 16 and pregnant. And now I'm going to hell.

We were still living in the two-bedroom house when I got pregnant. When the neighbors discovered I was pregnant, they started gossiping, saying it wasn't Fats' child. They were saying it was this other guy's child that liked me, and even had rumors out that they saw him jumping out of our living room window. And, of course, the story grew from there as they speculated on why he wouldn't leave out the front door. So once the news was out, as well as my belly, I went through that pregnancy with folks side-eyeing me and whispering behind my back. Fats' family didn't know what to believe. I wasn't close to them then, so it wasn't like we were communicating, and he was at college. So they waited it out while the gossip train continued running. As we reached the end of my term, I was ready to deliver this baby and shut all their mouths up.

Now back at home, my sister Tedda had assumed the role of head of household and was also the heart. I say that because Tedda had wisdom far beyond her age and always knew what to do in any situation. This knowledge would prove crucial one day when we were out shopping for groceries. Right in the middle of the cereal aisle, my water broke, but I had no clue what was happening. Again, going back to how we were raised, our complete sex education comprised the phrase, "don't let no boy touch you, or you're going to hell." Therefore, if there was never a discussion about sex, they sure enough weren't talking about delivering babies. So here I am, in the middle of the grocery store with what I thought was my bladder gone amok. I called out to Tedda, who was a little ahead of me, to come here. "Tedda, I don't know what's wrong, but I can't stop peeing." I had a dress on that day because nothing else fit anymore, and she lifted it a little and looked down my leg. And the liquid was still coming down. She busted out laughing, then looked at me real serious and said, "Your water broke, girl. You 'bout to have a baby."

So I said, "What do we do now? Do I go to the hospital?" She said, "No, we need to finish getting these groceries cause there's a sale on potatoes, and we need food in the house, and this sale's over today. Then we'll get you home, get you out of those "pee" clothes, pack you a bag and get you to the hospital. By then, you should be close." Just recalling this story brings a big smile to my face. I miss Tedda so much. She let nothing get her riled up. She was always calm and knew exactly what to do. And with her, it was always first things first. It's like she looked ahead ten steps before she decided what needed to be done.

Now I wasn't so calm. When we finally got home, and I changed my clothes, contractions had started. It's almost as if Tedda had predicted this because other than the water breaking, I felt nothing until after I had done everything she said. And boy, did that first contraction hit hard. My siblings were excited about the baby coming. Tedda and I proceeded to the hospital. Tangi stayed home till some of the other kids came home from school. So after only 2 hours of labor, I delivered my baby boy on a freezing day in January. Tedda called Fats' family for me, and they all came over. What I didn't know, and what confirmed this baby for them as Fats, is that all their family members were born with six fingers. This was an undeniable fact in their DNA, so it was plain as day when they brought my baby boy out, whom I named James after his daddy, and whom we called Jamo. After unwrapping him from all the swaddle blankets, I did what every mother does when she views her baby's body for the first time; I counted fingers and toes in front of them. Their walls of speculation went down as they happily embraced my baby boy. They showered him with love from that moment on.

***

After a few days in the hospital, I was back home. And with another mouth to feed in that 2-bedroom house, we desperately needed more space. After some searching in the area, my brother Carl, aka "Bug," who was a real adult and had a good job, came through with some money he had saved and bought a house that we could all live in on Prospect Street.

This house was exactly what we needed. All my siblings and I moved in. Tedda and her husband joined us, along with my other siblings, by Carl Dean. So that made about 15 of us, plus Jamo, in our new home.

Unfortunately, with all the ins and outs and especially all the kids, some nosey neighbors called Social Services on us. They ended up taking my siblings away once they realized there was no parent, at least of the kids, in the house. Tedda and her husband were of age, but they looked at me as a new mother needing help myself and wouldn't let me keep the kids in the house. They were sent to a foster home, which was more like a rooming house. They stayed with a lady named Ms. Ruby for just a couple of months because Tedda and I were determined to get our family back together. Besides, I had that promise in my head that I had made to my mother and Granny to always look after them. And as Carl Dean drilled in us, "We all we got."

After six months, we accomplished that feat. Jamo was getting bigger, and I was now 18 and had started back working. I saved some money, and Tedda and I went through the courts and fought to get our siblings back. With her being married and me having already raised them pretty much on my own, especially after Granny got sick, the judge saw no reason not to allow us to be together as long as the kids stayed in school and didn't get into any trouble. The court connected us with services, and we were able to get into some low-income housing at Simpson Manor. The best thing about these apartments was that they were townhouses, reasonably new, cheap, and two levels, with 2-4 bedrooms each - so we had plenty of room to spread out. I got one of the homes, and my sisters Doris, Sylvia, and Crystal came to live with me and helped with Jamo, plus my little brother Rooten was with me. My other sister Tanji also got a townhouse in the Manor and took our brothers to stay with her. My sister Tedda and her husband were already living at Simpson Manor. So we became one big family again at Simpson Manor for several years. And with all of us in the same location, we finally had some normalcy again.

As the years went on, my sister Doris, who is one year behind me, started dating and ended up moving out with her boyfriend. Eventually, everyone was doing their own thing, forming relationships and families. My brothers were now in their late teens, so that you couldn't tell them anything anyway. They were going to do what they wanted to do. Besides, they were happy to have their sisters leave the nest, especially to get some relief from multiple older sisters controlling their lives. Yep, my brothers were enjoying their freedom, and with so little to do now, I began to look for a place of my own. I had always dreamed of having my own house. It was a seed in my mind that grew while raising my siblings. Often when I looked around at that two-bedroom rental and even the house on Prospect Street, I knew I wanted more. I wanted greater than what I saw before me. I wanted to own my own home. I wanted the fairy tale with the big house, the white picket fence, the husband, the kid, and a dog. I now had a family. I just needed the place.

So I set out to find a house. It didn't take long at all. I found this wonderful house in Hiller, Pennsylvania, near where everyone else was living. Fats, Jamo, and I all moved in, and my fairy tale began. We were together, Jamo was growing up, and I was happy. I had always envisioned having my own family, except I didn't have the ring. I can still hear Granny's voice in my head about not doing anything with boys till you're married. I pushed that reminder aside because, in my mind, we were good. My little brother Paul stayed with us for a while but eventually moved back with Tanji. Lucy and I still hung out, and I was living my life. Also, an unfortunate result of not growing up with any parents during my teen years was that I had developed a mindset of "no one's gonna tell me what to do" or "you're not gonna tell me I can't do something." That was an understanding James and I had, considering how I grew up, and he didn't question it. He had a good job, was responsible, and cared for our needs.

Life went on, but cracks started to appear. Problems were occurring in our relationship. However, as far as I was concerned, Fats and I were good. But one day I came home and heard him on the phone. And he was talking to who I know was a woman because that's how he used to speak to me. I said nothing to him then, but I watched to see what else was happening. And my woman's intuition started showing me all the things my former naive and trusting self was missing. Unfortunately, you cannot unknow something once you know, and I started planning my exit. I didn't know why that was my first thought, especially since Fats had done nothing ever to hurt me physically. That was always a non-starter after what I saw with my mother and Carl Dean. However, I never wanted to be in a relationship where I had to question my man's loyalty, especially since I loved him so much.

I confronted him, and of course, he denied it. I told him, "I heard you tell another woman that you loved her." That was not going to work for me. This man, the only man I had ever known and loved, would not treat me like Carl Dean treated my mother. I was not about to keep pouring my love into someone who was with another woman. So I started planning how I was going to leave. Once I told him I was leaving, Fats didn't want to hear it. He was like, "you can't leave."

Now I don't know why he thought that meant anything to me. He knew better than anyone that I didn't do well with people telling me I couldn't do something. I've taken care of my siblings since I was 13 years old, and he was not about to tell me anything. This was my mentality at the time, and they were fighting words to him. I must have tapped something in his masculinity because he thought he needed to prove something to me. But considering I was not his wife, after all these years, there wasn't anything legally keeping me there. But then he got stupid and acted like he was going to hit me, and that was it. He didn't – but even the attempt doesn't need to happen but once. I'm done. And I did not care how much I loved him and always would; I was done.

I didn't leave immediately, but I did start getting all my stuff together. Growing up the way we did, I was not attached to much, so everything else could stay short of me and Jamo's clothes, toys, and games. I said nothing else to Fats. We were roommates at that point. He was barely coming home, anyway. It hurt like hell, but I left. I knew it was the right thing to do—my first love.

My Soul Cries Out

"Come to me, all ye that are heavy laden, and I will give you rest. Take my yoke upon you and learn from me; for I am meek and lowly In heart and ye shall find rest upon your souls. "For my yoke is easy, and my burden is light."

~Matthew 11:28-29

Once I had baby James or "Jamo" as we called him, Lucy, and I kind of fell off. Not because she had been one of the people pushing me to have sex, but because getting older, and my new responsibilities as a mother, naturally caused us to go in different directions. But her brother and one of my brothers remain good friends to this day. However, believe it or not, shy girl me gained another friend, Becky, who was a classmate of mine during my last years of high school. She would become my best friend through so much of my adult life.

Becky and I would hang out, and with or without a baby, we spent a lot of time together. Besides, I had a lot of babysitters, having been one most of my life for my sisters and brothers, so they were glad to repay the favor. One place we started hanging out was my uncle's club. This was my biological father's brother. The name of his club was The Diplomat. This is where I started working after Fisher's and Becky and I became hostesses there. Working here, I got to see what kind of man my father was, as well as his brother. Now, even though I say I never knew my bio father; I was aware of who he was. I remember a time while out shopping with my mother and she would point him out on the street and say, "that's your father, Moses Harris." But he never visited, came to see about us kids, or anything to show he cared. And that was that. Anyway, he and his brother were pretty much gangsters. People feared them.

Now people in our town who knew my parents say I look like both my mom and dad, while my sister looks just like our dad. I think the first time I officially met him was when Becky and I were out partying in the club. And it was then that he introduced me to his brother who owned the club, Uncle Slim. Uncle Slim would reach out to me all the time and we became close. I don't know why my father never did; it just never sat right with me that he never wanted to get to know me or his other kids. But what I did find out about him was that he had been shot several times. I didn't ask why.

But before that happened, and because I was working at Uncle Slim's club, I would see my father there. And he was high a lot. He asked if I wanted to get high with him. I said no, but I would still go see him because the little girl in me just wanted a relationship with her daddy. Later, I figured out why I needed to leave him alone. Some of his friends had been asking about me, talking about how pretty I was and everything, and how he needed to hook them up. So he was trying to pimp me out to his friends, saying how much good money I could make if I went out with some of these men. He would say, "All you gotta do is go to dinner with them. My partners been worrying me about you, and I was proud you was my daughter, you so pretty. Plus they're gonna pay off my debt for me. Just go to dinner with him, and he gonna break me off a piece." So this man, my biological father, was trying to pimp me out to his friends. Wow. That's all I can say.

***

After leaving Fats, I told Becky what had happened. By this time, Becky had stopped working at the club and had gotten married and moved to Virginia in the Tidewater area. Her husband Ronnie was in the military and stationed there. She told me to come stay with them in Virginia; they had extra room and that was all that needed to be said. Mind you, I had never been outside of my county, let alone another state. So, I gathered up Jamo, who was about eight years old then, and all I could fit in my red Pontiac Fiero. With my paper map unfolded to Virginia, we left Brownsville, PA, and set off for our new life.

I know God gave me the strength to make that move because once we arrived, I was determined to be at Becky's home only for about 30 days, as grateful as I was for the hospitality. My son needed his own space, and I never wanted to be in a position where he couldn't be free to be a kid. So within a day or two of settling in, I landed a job at Red Lobster working as a waitress. And true to my goal, in 30 days, I had earned enough money to get my own place. I remember that day so well. The only furniture I had was a wicker chair, but it was enough. It was mine.

I loved our new home, and I was gradually acquiring the things we needed, like beds and other furniture. And the best part of the job at Red Lobster was that I could walk there. Jamo and I were getting accustomed to our new area, and he was making some friends. There were also a few stores the kids would go to after school as well as the local McDonald's up the street.

Now in the area we lived, back in the '80's, groups of gangs started forming throughout different neighborhoods causing a lot of havoc in the Tidewater area, mainly as a result of drug dealing and the rising crack epidemic going on up and down the East Coast. One day, when Jamo was about 10, he went to McDonald's with his friends after school. Some gang members surrounded them and demanded their tennis shoes when they were leaving. Jamo told him "no" and they pulled a gun on him.

He did give up the shoes, but I freaked out after hearing what happened. I knew I had to make a decision right then, as I had heard these gangs didn't stop at just stealing your shoes off your feet, they were into some serious things, even attempted murders. I decided to call his father. I knew Jamo would be okay back home and Fats could teach him how to protect himself from things I could not. I also did not want to be one of those mothers who allow their son to be in jeopardy just because I needed him to be with me. I knew I could only protect him so far, especially with my varied work hours. So to keep my son safe, Fats and I arranged for Jamo to live with him.

This decision was the most difficult thing I have had to overcome since the passing of my mother and grandmother. I just could not reconcile the fact that after raising all my siblings, I wasn't able to raise my own child. And I still had my mom's voice and even Carl Dean's voice in my head saying, "We all we got." I felt guilty. In fact I felt a plethora of emotions. I knew it was the best thing for him. I knew I couldn't keep him there and take a chance of something happening to him because, well, I didn't even want to think about what could happen. My heart was broken. First my mom, then Granny and now Jamo.

[Note: You might be wondering why I say Carl Dean so much, when he was my dad? I can't even tell you why, it's just something we all did as siblings. We all called him Carl Dean. Additionally, I don't understand nor will I ever understand his relationship with my mother; I do know now that they both loved each other in their own way and I respect that. I also saw that Carl Dean loved every last one of us kids as well. His final words before passing as he's whispered in our ears was, "Stay together; we all we got." I'm so happy I was able to come to terms with his place in our lives and provide forgiveness and love for my dad, Carl Dean before he passed.]

Living To Die

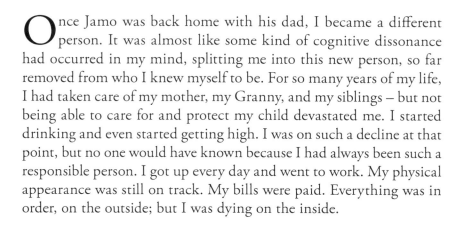

"Through my tears, I found God in myself, and I loved her fiercely."

~Ntozake Shange

Once Jamo was back home with his dad, I became a different person. It was almost like some kind of cognitive dissonance had occurred in my mind, splitting me into this new person, so far removed from who I knew myself to be. For so many years of my life, I had taken care of my mother, my Granny, and my siblings – but not being able to care for and protect my child devastated me. I started drinking and even started getting high. I was on such a decline at that point, but no one would have known because I had always been such a responsible person. I got up every day and went to work. My physical appearance was still on track. My bills were paid. Everything was in order, on the outside; but I was dying on the inside.

I'm in tears now remembering how much I missed my son. A gusher of grief washed over me recalling how I never had time to fully mourn the death of my mother or Granny. I just had to pick up the pieces and keep going. As a result, I had grown this shell around my heart, this veneer of hardness to take care of my siblings, but that outer shell was like an egg now, cracks were showing, and once I had to let Jamo live with his dad, that was the final breaking. I was done.

I was alone. My only companions were these rushing emotions that I just did not want to deal with. So alcohol and drugs became the cover, the solace in the truth of my life I kept bumping up against. And the truth was, I was hurt and depressed, and I didn't know how to release the pain. I questioned everything. "Why was my life like this? Why do the people I love keep getting taken away from me? All these questions continually bombarded my soul, while the devil had the time of his life. He was throwing darts of doubt and fear in my mind, causing me to question every decision I made up to that point. And it was working. I didn't know any specifics, but I know he was trying to kill, steal and destroy every part of my life. And all the while these thoughts were coming, I was thinking about how I was supposed to make my mom proud. At this point I wasn't sure that I had. I knew I took care of my siblings and did the best I knew how, and everyone was fine; but why was I falling apart?

I thought I had made it.

I had envisioned this Barbie doll photogenic image of the happy family, with me as Barbie, Fats as Ken, and baby Jamo. I had latched onto James and loved him with all my heart. We had our house, our stability, and I had the ideal life. Until it crashed. Gone was the picture-perfect life. I started drinking to try and get the picture of my ideal life back in focus. I started smoking to do the same. But the more I drank and the more I smoked, the more blurry everything became. I didn't want to look back, and I definitely didn't want to look ahead. I wanted my life back the way it was. So as long as I stayed right there in the moment, focusing on my perfect picture, I could cope. I could get up every day and get dressed and get to work. I'm Debbie. I'm responsible. I can do it all. But I knew if I looked away, away from that picture, for just a second - I was gonna see the truth. I was going to see reality and Nope, not gonna see it. Not gonna feel that. I'm good. I'm good. I'm good!!!!!

As that first year away from Jamo sank in, I had fallen further into a dark place. There was no one around who truly understood me. "How could they?" I asked. They never experienced any of the traumas that I had gone through. My current life was not something that I was proud of, or something that I really want to share. However, God was tenderly affirming to me that what I was going through was not about me. It was about bringing value to someone else's life and allowing them to see just how good God is. He was trying to show me that He will take your darkest moments, and the things that you thought you never would get through, the thing that had you so bound that you stopped living life and were just existing – and bring you out. That's the place I was. But I did not want to leave yet. And so, that revelation was slow coming because I had trained myself to live a lie. Remember, I had mastered keeping up the façade. I had to be the strong one.

So drinking heavily, I did all kinds of drugs, and went out clubbing every chance I could. But I always made it to work the next day. I was clearly working those two sides of me. There was the professional Debbie who always had it together at work; and the party girl who appeared after working hours. I'll never forget one night I was out at a club, by myself, which I did often and didn't mind. I was sitting at the bar having a drink and this man sat down beside me. His exact words were, "My dad told me when you go out, look for the most beautiful woman in the club. I guarantee you she's the loneliest woman there." Of course I shut him down because he was right (at least about me being lonely), and I didn't want to have to talk to or deal with him asking me any questions, fearing the sadness would come out.

Man that devil was working hard to destroy my life and he was succeeding. If I never looked at the truth, talked to anyone, or owned up to how I was feeling – I would stay right where he wanted me. I was on the road to self-destruction without knowing it. Satan had convinced me I was going to die young anyway, just like my mom.

That night I remember crying out to God, "How much pain can one heart take!" Then I thought to myself, "Alright girl, you're still alive. What are you going to do to honor your mom's death???" Those thoughts got me through so many devastating times in my life. I was depressed and didn't know it. And to be honest, though I continued to show up for work, I was a walking, dysfunctional mess. But God!!!

Knowing my pain so well, and being the loving God He is, God orchestrated four Angels into my life: Shona, Louise, Claudia, and Jackie. You know God is with you when he sends you not one, but four powerful sister friends. Real friends, ride-or-die friends. My girl Shona has a heart of gold. When she loves you, she loves deep. But don't get it twisted, she's that friend that's also going to tell you the truth even when it hurts. God knows I needed that!! Louise is my everything Angel, full of wisdom and understanding. Claudia is my sister-in-law who I've loved from the first day we met. My girl when I said "Let's … , she said "Go!" She knew I needed someone to look out for me, as I was out there drinking and driving. She knew all of our family issues and loved not just me but our entire family without judgment. And rounding out the group is Jackie. Jackie is one of the strongest women I know, my praying friend from day one. Jackie would always invite me to church; but during this period, church was the furthest thing from my mind. But these were my girls. I was so blessed to have them, especially not having my mom in my life to navigate the different seasons of womanhood. And these women loved me fiercely. And I am very aware how unusual it is to have so many women to love you and be a fantastic front row, to honor and celebrate you, and also hold you accountable.

Regrettably my steely façade was effective at hiding my depression for a long time, although the ladies knew something was wrong with me because they would question why I was getting drunk all the time. But they pushed it away since they thought of me as so confident; they even remarked how if in a relationship and the man does one thing wrong, I will act like he never existed. They actually looked at that as a good thing; but it was not. I was suppressing how I felt. I was dismissing my emotions because I could not afford to have those feelings in my space. I only knew how to move on.

Besides, who was coming to my rescue? The independent attitude wasn't something I necessarily decided on, it was decided for me. I had no options. When mom died, then Granny — I was an orphan child raising seven other orphans. There was no other way to be. Now, I loved that the ladies saw me that way, that warrior in me; but it was definitely overrated. I needed help.

***

As the polished Debbie continued working at the restaurant, I started running into a lot of men trying to get my number or ask me out. It felt strange even going out on a date or communicating with another man on a romantic level. I had only been with one man my entire life, so I didn't even know how to date. Consequently, when I met someone that I was interested in, I got attached quickly. I also left quickly. I wanted so desperately to be loved that if I didn't feel any love for the other person immediately, I would end the relationship or stop the communication. I couldn't stand to feel that type of hurt from a man again. I would forget about them so quickly just like they never even existed. I didn't know it then, but I was searching for someone to love me the way I loved and had given all my love to my ex.

After being away from Fats for a while, I had gotten extremely good at coping, without my son to love and to love me, and went about trying to be everything to everyone. I thought if I could give all of me, or all of my love to my friends and male companions and be everything they needed, they would have to love me. Unfortunately, that made me the person that everybody else wanted me to be. As I became the dependable one to everyone else, I started progressively losing myself. All of my efforts ended up in tears and disappointment time after time. I felt emotionally tormented about the future and unconsciously started putting myself in dangerous situations.

I would go to the clubs the minute I got off work on Friday evenings and party all weekend. I would call my girls to see if they were coming, but if not, it never stopped me. I would go by myself. I was used to doing things by myself anyway, so this just fit in with my mindset. Besides it was the only thing I knew to do that would stop the thoughts trying to take over in my head. I didn't need any communication with anyone. I would just drink and imagine that ultimate dream I always wanted - the beautiful girl married to her prince, with their beautiful children beside them, living in a big house.

Then just when the alcohol and the imaginations were finally getting in sync, I would remember how I was separated once again from Fats, and that we were never getting back together. So I would get another drink. Then I'd remember all the sacrifices I had made to raise my siblings after Momma and Granny died. And how I wanted to make them proud. And as I sat there drinking, I remember never even having a break to just stop and grieve, or be a teenager, or even to be married cause the picture would not stay in focus.

Then of course, that devil would come with his lie again about me dying young. He wanted me to believe that since my mother died at 33 years old from high blood pressure, I was next in line. I had already been diagnosed with high blood pressure and was told it was hereditary. Therefore, in my mind, no one could say to me that I was not going to die young. This self-sabotaging behavior continued for years until I met the man I thought was the answer to all my prayers, someone I thought would take away all the pain from the past. I was convinced that all the prayers my friends had been praying for me for years to meet someone had finally come to pass. I was confident this man was the answer.

After dating for two years, we were married on my mother's birthday, September 20th. Mother's Day, my mom's birthday, and Christmas were always holidays where I would get depressed before that date— just thinking about not having my mom kept me in that low place for weeks. But then this amazing man, whom I believed God sent, had come into my life to change all that. I wanted to believe in that fairytale so much. However, God will always show us that you can't put your happiness, joy, deliverance, healing, and peace in no one other than Him. But, of course, my husband did not know that was my expectation. It was not my husband's responsibility to be everything for me. He didn't even know anything about these ideas of mine. That was my responsibility. Needless to say, our marriage was destined to fail. I married a fantastic man; however, I was not healed or whole, and our marriage ended after five years and two beautiful children.

Now, again, I am packing up my home with two kids. I was so shattered. I hated moving out of our lovely, comfortable single-family home on the water, back into an apartment. But I was determined to give my children a good life. I did not have time to concern myself with another relationship's death. I had to survive for my children's sake. However, I could not outrun the emptiness, shame, hurt, pain, and depression awaiting me again. I thought I had it all neatly tucked away, but here they were, waiting to overwhelm me again if I just gave up.

But I did not give up. Instead, I intentionally pushed those emotions back where they belonged and secured a job as an Assistant Store Manager at Burlington Coat Factory. I also worked off-hours in a network marketing business called Prepaid Legal. Although my children didn't want for anything, I lived my life in trepidation, waiting for the next trauma, the next bad event. I had no peace, just a foreboding fear of the future.

***

Looking back on my life, all I ever wanted was to be married, have children, and live happily ever after. I didn't think about having a career. My career would've been raising my children in a loving, caring, supportive, healthy home. That was my dream. And now, my children are being taken away from their father, and our home is split up. And I'm starting all over again. When I looked in the mirror, I didn't like what I saw. I didn't like that woman staring back at me. To me, that woman is a failure. That's how I saw myself. And I felt like a failure because I was failing my children.

Those negative emotions came because I was working so many hours that I did not have sufficient time to raise my children. "What type of mother am I?" These guilty thoughts kept me broken and ashamed. I told myself so many lies about my worth, how I wasn't good enough, or allowed others to say I wasn't good enough. And those feelings did not leave when others treated me disrespectfully. Although I believed I could run through brick walls and battle for others, I couldn't do the same for myself. At one point, I felt used. Everybody I tried to love abandoned me.

What is wrong with me?

Do I not deserve to be loved?

It was as if I was in a prison where no love could remain. And although it may not have been a physical prison, it was definitely a mental one. I was holding unforgiveness in my heart against those who had harmed me, and I had never healed from the trauma of losing my mother and grandmother at such an early and pivotal age in my development. My capacity to continue to carry all of this weight was weakening. I had taken on the superwoman persona for so long but it was heavy. I wanted to let it go. I wanted to feel at peace.

Was that too much to ask?

I did not know what to do.

I was paralyzed with fear, not even wanting to get out of bed. But I had my kids to think about. So, not only did I get up, but I smiled, and no one knew what I was hiding behind that smile. And since my heart was broken, once again I went looking for love. I began to date this man, a type of man I would never bring home in front of my children. But I brought him home, and I moved him in. This is when my Angels knew I'd lost my mind. If anyone knew me, it was these ladies, and they knew for a fact that I would never bring a man I wasn't serious about in front of my children no matter what.

This behavior was definitely out of character for me. I was very protective of my children, even with their fathers, but this man had no connection to us. I mean, we weren't even engaged, let alone married. Yet I moved this man in with us as all of my friends kept asking, "What are you doing, Debbie? I can't believe you're letting him move in with you." That's when I started feeling like I was on a fast road to hell. Looking at myself in the mirror one morning, I couldn't believe where I was, nor did I like it. I had to ask myself, "What am I doing? Why did I bring this man in my house? I don't do that. That's not me!"

I was at my ultimate low point by this time. And it was weird at the same time too. You know how there are certain people who are known for certain things, good or bad. For instance, I can hear God saying, "I expect that from Tangi or Tina, but I don't expect that from you, Debbie." God knows who we are and what we're made of. He knows our gifts and talents. He knows what he's put in us, and he knows the things that'll break us too. I mean I'm the kind of person who never wanted to smoke anything cause I thought I might end up a drug addict.

So at this point in my life, I had a man living with me and my children and there has been absolutely no discussion of marriage. One evening at a party we threw for one of my friends, all the shame and negativity I felt about myself rose up while I was watching everyone in the room. Looking at this man, I was like, "he's just a boyfriend but I let him move in." I really had hit rock bottom. All my friends were like, "He's not even your type. Yes, I see that he loves you. Yes, I know he'll do anything for you; however, that has never been you." But I was tired. I was worn out. I was tired of being the super one. I was tired of hiding behind a fake smile. I wanted freedom, and I wanted it bad.

My friends could see that I couldn't hold it together anymore. I can't remember which friend gave me this videotape, but someone gave me No More Sheets by Juanita Bynum, the gospel singer, author, and pastor. As I watched that video, I cried like a baby. That following Sunday, I called my friend Jackie and told her to pick me up for church. I never expected to see what I saw.

We pulled up to the church, got out of the car, and had to wait in line to get inside the church. So I began to make jokes, to cover my fear of walking inside that church. My nerves were entirely on edge. I told Jackie, "I've waited in a club in lines, but I have never waited in a line to go to a church." That scared me. But I tell you, it was one of the best decisions I ever made in my life. The church, Calvary Revival Bible Church, was in Norfolk, Virginia.

Chapter 5

Beauty For Ashes (Salvation, Bishop McBath, Pastor Duncan)

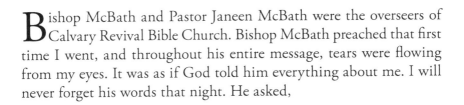

To bestow on them a crown of beauty instead of ashes, the oil of joy instead of mourning,
and a garment of praise instead of a spirit of despair'

~ISAIAH 61:3

Bishop McBath and Pastor Janeen McBath were the overseers of Calvary Revival Bible Church. Bishop McBath preached that first time I went, and throughout his entire message, tears were flowing from my eyes. It was as if God told him everything about me. I will never forget his words that night. He asked,

"Is someone in here that's been on a merry-go-round the majority of their adult life, and constantly looking for love in all the wrong places? She's been trying to find love in men and male friends, looking for a man to replace the father she never had. She's going

to the gym working out; she's even been buying new furniture but can't get the house like she wants it. She smiles, but behind that smile no one knows what she still wants but her and God. This woman that is in here today has tried everything else looking for unconditional love. But I say to you woman, now that you have tried everything else, I dare you to try Jesus!"

As I sat there in awe listening to this man tell all my business, somehow my feet began to move. I ended up standing in the front of the altar with Pastor Janeen's hands over my shoulders praying. While she prayed for me I crumbled to the floor. I don't remember falling, but that's what Jackie told me I did.

After finally getting myself together after that experience, I went home and asked my friend – the man I had moved in with me - to move out. I still cannot believe I did that especially since he and I were good. I literally got home from church and abruptly told him he had to go. He thought I was trippin', just going through something, and to be honest, it did take a whole month before he would move out. And the only reason he finally did move out was because from that time on, I refused to sleep in the same bed with him. I made him sleep on the couch, and I slept in the bed. He initially dismissed my new stance, trying to accommodate me tripping, he thought. However, I still went to church every Sunday, and Wednesdays too now, until he saw that this was the new me, and finally moved out. And on another Sunday, right before he left, I was blessed with the infilling of the Holy Spirit and speaking in tongues.

The manifestation of my change was immediate. When I got home from church that day I had such a fire for the Lord that I threw away all the alcohol and cigarettes that were in my house. I even went through my closet and bagged up all the provocative clothes that I had been wearing and took them down to the dumpster. My girlfriends were upset with me because they felt I should have at least given them to them. However, I knew in my spirit that God was telling me to throw them away so I could not give them to anybody. I threw away all my secular music as well because I thought at the time I couldn't listen to it and focus on my relationship with God.

Then the following day something happened that shook me to my knees. I began to throw up continually. I couldn't understand what was going on. It felt like one of those times when you drink too much and have a hangover the next day, because I was throwing up and throwing up. I was so sick that I called my pastor and shared with him what was going on. "I don't know what's happening," I told him, "but I promise you I haven't drank anything. I feel like I'm having a hangover experience," I told him. The pastor told me that God was purging me.

This experience caused a complete pivot in my life. I became a fully devoted, completely sold-out follower of Jesus Christ. My life was my job, my kids and my Jesus. Nothing else mattered. For the next two years, as I totally committed my life to Christ, I would finally experience that peace that surpasses all understanding.

Once I gave my life to Christ, I was all in. I figured since I had gone extremely hard for the devil, surely I can go extremely hard for Christ now. And anyone who knows me knows - when I give myself to something - I give myself totally and completely. I immediately signed up for this advanced course in understanding God for the next six months. I started serving in ministry. I was learning how to walk like Jesus and talk like Jesus. To hear me tell it, with all I was learning, my zeal for the Lord was on 1,000. My "understanding" was so high that I knew I was only hearing straight from God himself and I could tell others what He was saying.

As I was growing in the things of the Lord, I would meet a minister at church named Minister Epps. I always called him Minister, to the point my youngest son Isiah thought Minister Epps' first name was Minister. He was very instrumental to my growth in Christ that one day, having observed me for some time and how on fire I was for the Lord, told me he felt that God sent him to be my husband. Now this is a man who has been in Christ for years. But me, the new, wholly bold Jesus is my Best Friend Debbie told Minster Epps, "God sent you to help me learn how to love Him, not you." I was very clear without any hesitation. He just looked at me like "who do you think you are." I even had the nerve to tell him, "I also don't think you're fasting enough as a minister because if you're only fasting until lunch, anybody could do that." Whew, the audacity.

Nonetheless, for the next two years I amazed myself at how hard I went for the Lord. Fortunately my zeal tampered down a bit, and Minister Epps and I were able to laugh about the whole situation and become real friends. From that day forward, I finally started settling down and for the time since before my mother died, I relished in my peace. And it was the real kind, the kind that only Jesus can give you. The kind you just cannot explain. And I was enjoying it tremendously. Now when I smiled, it was for real. There was nothing behind that smile but joy. I felt good about myself. I felt pure.

Chapter 6
All In and All Out
(Throwing Up All The Past)

 "We may encounter many defeats, but we must not be defeated."
~Maya Angelou

Over the next few years, I grew in my faith and love of the Lord and also in my commitment to the church. In this environment, I was more joyous than I had been since prior to my mother's passing. I even changed the way I was raising my kids. I stopped them from watching certain things on TV, even monitored the music they were listening to. Like I said, I went all in. I implemented a lot of do's and don'ts, and even had my daughter participate in an abstinence ceremony at the church in which she and the other girls were symbolically married to Christ. We got her a ring and everything. I wanted her to know why she was saving herself, not just the fear that had been instilled in me, but because she was a precious jewel in God's eyes and did not belong to just anyone.

In addition to participating in service at my home church, I attended events at a number of different churches with my church family. At one particular church, someone prophesied to me, saying "You haven't met your husband yet, but you're going to meet him soon. And when you meet him, he's gonna ask you a question."

So now I'm excited. I was still young, and still pretty quiet, but because I love, love, love even the idea of love, I was hopeful. And of course, I loved the idea of being married. That was part of my ideal life. So about three weeks after this prophecy was relayed to me, there was a gentleman named Gregory Alford, who was waiting in line with me and some other members to attend a class at my church. While waiting, Gregory came up to me and said, "Excuse me?" Now remember they said you haven't met him yet, and as I turned around I knew I had never seen this man before. So turning, I said "Yes?" He asked me, "Do you know what time it is?" I told him the time and then we started talking since we were still waiting to go into the class. He asked how long I had been at the church, and he said he had been there many years. He asked me about the class, and I shared how excited I was in my new life in Christ and all I was being taught by Bishop McBath. He then asked for my number. Then we started talking regularly. Then I remembered the prophecy!!! The man I was to marry would ask me a question. Y'all know I was immediately thinking could this be it! I was like, "Oh my God, he's been in this church all this time. I haven't ever seen him. He asked me a question. God, the prophecy is being fulfilled right now." So I was off to the races, excited about what was happening.

Now some time passes, and the Lord reminded me several times that I was His and I needed to represent Him in all I do. So as Greg and I continued to see each other, we shared our love of travel and made plans to go on a cruise. While on the boat, we booked separate cabins. I was determined that nobody would touch my body anymore unless I was married. And I meant that with my entire soul. So we did all these vacations together and kept everything above board and godly.

Soon thereafter, Greg asked me to marry him, and I said Yes!!! Greg and I got engaged, but it was so funny because he would often hear me quoting Bishop pretty much every day and on so many different subjects. I would be like, "Well Bishop said... and Bishop said." It got to the point where he was even saying to me, "Well what did Bishop say about this..." And it usually was about how we conducted ourselves when alone, but he said that to the whole church. He knew how the flesh will always win when your guard is down. Bishop would tell us ladies especially, "He gotta get out of your house by a certain time cause "things" start happening the later it gets." I would tell Greg, "just call me Cinderella 'cause you got to go by midnight."

So the relationship was progressing nicely. However, the long hours I was still working were causing me to feel guilty about the little quality time I had with my children. Because of this, I didn't make them do any chores at the house. I would work all day and then come home and clean their rooms or just clean the house. I never would get on them about anything. But there came a particular time when I had locked the door with my keys still inside. I called Greg and asked him to come over. He came and broke a window and got inside. Once in, as he walked through the house, he saw how the kids' rooms were in shambles. Now the rest of the house was fine, but I immediately said "Oh, excuse the kids' room." He said, "Oh no. I know the way you work as a single mother. I'm surprised you even got any of your house cleaned." But this was only the calm before the storm. What he said next was "If you don't mind, I'll help you clean it, alright?" "Knock yourself out," I responded. When I got home later that day, the house was spotless. And I don't mean clean, I mean spotless - as if no one had ever lived there. That should have been the first red flag; but it was not. Mainly because I was thinking, "somebody cleaning my house, yeah that'll work for me."

But there was another red flag, and this occurred right after we set our date to get married. While on our way to get the marriage license, Greg informs me he never got divorced from his first wife. He said the paperwork never went through to his knowledge. I asked him if he had completed paperwork to get a divorce. He responded, "Yes, I signed the papers and sent them back to her; but she never sent them back."

??????

What I found out was his "wife" was angry over something that had occurred between them, and she was intent on taking him through all these changes in order to prove her point before signing the papers. As a result, we had to delay our wedding a whole year. I'm thinking to myself, "Ok, here we go." But that was the Lord making sure things happened properly.

Nonetheless, before we were married, Greg and I went through six months of pre-marital counseling with Bishop McBath. During that time, Bishop told Greg,

> "As you come into this marriage, let Deborah be the head of the house at first. Any issues you have with the kids, you need to bring them straight to her initially because she has been in this role of superwoman and on her own since she was 13. This is the only way she knows how to manage, and she is going to have to ease into letting you be the head. Don't come in and try to take over right away. It won't work. You need to first develop a relationship with her kids so they can learn to trust you, because if you go in and start disciplining them, it's going to be a problem. Just communicate everything to your wife until everyone adjusts and you all will be fine."

So we got through the counseling, but on the day of the wedding I started having serious pre-wedding jitters. It was so bad that Jackie, who was my maid of honor - the one that prayed for me – was greatly concerned and left to get Bishop. He came into the room and saw me hyperventilating uncontrollably. He then asked me, "Are you sure you wanna do this Deborah, because it's never too late? Are you absolutely sure you want to do this?" I was still tripping and all over the place emotionally, but mustered up enough strength to say, "Yes." But that Yes had so many red flags attached to it in my spirit that it was laughable. And it wasn't just a red flag, but a red-hot fire engine, mini-skirt, Louboutin red bottom shoes red, red flag - but I was still going forward. And so we got married and the shenanigans started immediately during the reception.

In Genesis 2:24 (NIV), the scripture says, "Therefore a man leaves his father and his mother and cleaves to his wife, and they become one flesh." But the man I had just married was with his mom the entire night during the reception. And as we were on our way to the hotel in our limousine, he stopped the driver and got out and said. "I need to make sure my mom's OK with me leaving." I'm sorry. What just happened??? The backstory of this "godly" relationship is that we had been dating for three whole years and then spent another year waiting on his divorce papers, and after all that, the most important thing for you is not getting to finally sees your wife in the flesh but to check with your mother to see if you can leave? "What did I just sign up for?" I asked myself.

Now a little backstory to show how we can sometimes convince ourselves of something despite what we're seeing with our own eyes. Initially, I was OK with Greg's relationship with his mother while we were dating, especially since she was old. In fact, I kind of envied it because I always imagined that's how my mother and I would be. Anyway, after making sure she was good, we finally left for the honeymoon. Once we got back home, since I had a house and Greg had an apartment, he moved in with me, Irene, and Isiah.

It is now day three into our new life and Irene and Isiah were staying with their dad that particular evening. I decided to light some candles, put some music on and slip into this beautiful white sexy lingerie, and wait for my man to come home. Once I heard his key in the door, I stood up with my heels in one hand and the other hand on my hip, and a smile on my face. His face lit up and broke out into this huge smile. He was like "You look so amazing. This is so nice. Let me put my stuff down." He quickly goes into the kitchen to put his lunch container and everything in it in the sink. He notes that the dishes were washed but the sink was not cleaned out. He then walked into the living room where I was patiently waiting and said, "Who washed the dishes?"

Throwing me off my good mood, I was like, " Why?" Well that good deed went left extremely fast. Greg got this strange look on his face then said, "Who does that? Who washes dishes without cleaning out the sink? That is just ridiculous !" And he went on and on about it. Now I'm standing there confused because I thought that I was going to take his mind off of everything but me, and now the night turned into an argument and poked out lips.

Things got progressively worse that evening as he continued nagging about what Irene and Isiah were not doing correctly as far as he was concerned. He felt they didn't make their beds right, Isiah didn't take out the trash, Irene left hair in the sink when she combed her hair for school, and on and on some more. Needless to say, that crazy night ended in disgust. But gotta move on I'm thinking. Just a little bump. This marriage has to work.

Then a few months later, after going for my routine mammogram three months into our marriage, I was told they saw a spot on the imaging and needed me to get a biopsy. The biopsy came back positive. I was diagnosed with Stage 1 Breast Cancer. I was devastated. And my new husband in Christ could not even console me. He just stopped communicating. All he cared about was that the house was 100% spotless.

I went to church to talk to Bishop about this and he assigned us with some marriage couple counselors. Marriage counseling was literally a waste of time. Greg would not talk to the couple either, and all I did was cry. I am more miserable now than I was before we got married because in my mind I'm thinking *this marriage is in Christ, it's got to work. Jesus is at the center, right?*

So not only did our marriage get off to a rocky start, but it was quickly devolving. I was so hurt. But something about this hurt felt different. Even in our daily interactions, I had never been treated so cold as by my new husband. He was just not emotionally there. Now I'm not saying he was a bad man, but what I later realized was that we were both broken souls and when you bring together two halves in Christ, it does not make a whole. However, I was so perplexed as to how this could be if I'm living for Jesus. I did everything right, didn't I? But then again, I was still a babe in Christ I reasoned. So I began to blame Jesus in my head, thinking, "Yeah, he's a man too. All men do is hurt you. That's what they do. Jesus took my mom away and that was the worst pain I could ever experience. And after all that, I do everything you ask me to do and all I get is hurt again."

Things only got worse. I was so disappointed. After all those years of waiting and finally walking down the aisle with a Christian man.

Chapter 7

Nothing Left (Internal Fight)

> When we shrink from the sight of something, when we shroud it in euphemism, that is usually a sign of inner conflict, of unsettled hearts, a sign that something has gone wrong in our moral reasoning.
>
> ~MATTHEW SCULLY

Greg still hated that after working two jobs, I would come home and clean. He was the type of man where everything in the home had to be clean, and nothing could be out of place. He was so obsessed with order, that one day he called me at work and asked me why the toilet paper on the roll was hung in the wrong direction. I was like, "What? I've never heard that before." Another incident occurred with my daughter. She wanted me to be happy, so she decided to help out and wash the dishes, put everything away and clean up the kitchen for me. She was very excited to show me when I got home. Greg got home first, and she excitedly told him, "Mr. Greg, I washed the dishes and cleaned up the kitchen." He was like, "Oh, great job," then he went to the kitchen and saw that the sink again wasn't wiped out.

An instant change occurred in his demeanor and in his facial expression. He went from being ok to eerily quiet, so my daughter came to me as I arrived shortly thereafter and said "Mr. Greg is mad at me. I thought he was gonna be happy because I washed the dishes." I told her "Don't worry about it," I then asked him what was going on. "What is wrong with you?" I asked. "Why didn't you give her a little praise?" He said, "I just don't understand. How can anyone wash dishes and leave the sink dirty?" "Are you kidding me?" I said. My daughter heard his response and later came to me and said, "Mom, can I just go and live with my dad."

Now remember, because I worked so many hours on as many as two and a half jobs just to take care of them the way I wanted and felt they deserved, I felt guilty about not spending so much time with them, so I didn't make them do any chores in the house. This was completely unacceptable to my husband, but it definitely went far beyond that. And whatever his upbringing, his military training, or just his own warped sense of order, it completely alienated my children. Greg especially did not like that these kids, as old as they were, did not regularly do chores around the house.

So initially after what Greg said to my daughter I thought, *she's just upset right now.* However, after that incident and in the following days I would come home from work and knew things were not right. The atmosphere in the house had such a presence of gloom and doom over it. When I walked in, you could see how anxious my kids had become. And although I was always tired when I got home from work, seeing them was my joy and when they saw me, it was their joy as well. And we had created such a wonderful life together and now this man, who I thought was going to come and make us better as a family, was ripping us all apart. And each time I walked in the door from work, the atmosphere felt like death. No one was smiling, no one was happy. Everyone was miserable.

My children didn't want to live with me anymore. They kept asking me over and over again if they could go live with their dad.

No God.

Please.

I felt my heart breaking into a million pieces.

This was the final straw.

This was what caused me to snap, to finally let go of reality, and lose my reason for living.

My children told me that life in our house, with my husband, had gotten so bad that they wanted to go live with their father.

And now, once again, I have to make a decision concerning my kids' happiness and security.

I still cry thinking about it. How did I get here? Why am I again considering sending my kids to live with their father? What kind of mother am I and how did I get to a place where my babies no longer want to be with me? This was my lowest point ever. All because I married this man, and now our lives are falling apart.

Things escalated downwards quickly from there. Again, after only three months of marriage and a cancer diagnosis we're sent to marriage counseling and my husband not only refuses to participate but completely abandons me during my illness. So sending my kids away took me over the edge. I didn't want to be with him anymore. I didn't want to be in Hampton anymore. I didn't want to be anywhere.

Now at the time, the retail store where I worked was considered a "best methods" store. Every single entity in my store had a best method and because of that, my reputation for hitting our store goals made me a standout in the district. As a result, I was chosen as a regional representative to travel to other store locations to help them get in line with best methods by modeling the practices and procedures I had put into place and implemented with all of my store employees.

However, as well as my store and employees were doing, I was completely falling apart. This personal situation in my life was becoming too much, and I needed a change. And although my District Manager (DM) looked to me as a consistent and strong support in his district, I went to him that same week and said I needed to relocate; that I needed to get out of Hampton. I told him that due to some critical emotional things going on in my life, I would need to take a leave of absence.

I needed help.

I had to get away from there.

Fortunately, I had such a close relationship with my DM, that when he looked into my face, he immediately said, "I'm getting you out of here. Take the next two weeks and do whatever you need to do for you." He would later transfer me to an A.J. Wright store in Alexandria, Virginia – several hours away, but he knew I needed time to get my head together. (To this day, I have a very close relationship with Eric, and we still stay in touch.)

So I left and went home. As I sat on the couch contemplating this situation, my thoughts led me to a new place. I knew I had messed up. I needed to fix this. My children were gone, and the marriage was over. All of my hopes and dreams were now gone. Everything I wanted had evaporated due to my own choices. And here I was. Five years later. With nothing.

So I went to my happy place, my safe place, the place I go to talk with God. I went to the beach. You know water has such a calming and soothing effect on so many people. I love being at or by the water. So off I went. It wasn't that far away, and I went there to get some solace. To get some peace from all the trauma I was experiencing in this marriage that I thought was from God.

After I drove to the beach and parked, I got out and started walking in the sand towards the water. I was just looking ahead. Walking into the ocean. All I can remember after that is my girlfriend grabbing me and pulling me back. I don't remember how she got there or how she even knew where I was. And I don't remember thinking I wanted to die. But I also don't know how to swim. Yet I was walking straight into the water. It had gotten about waist high when I felt these hands grabbing me and holding me tight, calmly saying, "Let's go."

Chapter 8

Getting To Peace
(Therapy: You Need To Talk
It Out)

We may encounter many defeats, but we must not be defeated.
~Maya Angelou

I didn't think I wanted to take my life. But walking into the ocean that summer day said otherwise. I could not swim and yet I was waist-high in the ocean without a life vest or a buoy. Just my body walking on its own into the water, not thinking or even feeling anything at all. Just numb.

God sent an angel that day to rescue me. No one knew I was even there. I had called no one, yet God knew. He knows all. And He knows me. Deborah. He knew where I was and what I was feeling, and He wanted to make sure that I knew that day that I was loved. That He was thinking about me and that He loved me with an unfailing love and would do whatever it took to come rescue me. Although in my heart I felt God's love, I was battling some deep-rooted traumas that had me going back and forth about God's love for me and my self-worth.

I was so hurt at the state of my life.

How did I allow myself to get here?

Once my DM transferred me out of Hampton and into a new place in Alexandria, Virginia, God came to my rescue again. He added therapy to my path towards healing. In fact, I needed therapy to make sense of it all.

In 2007, as I began therapy, this was the state of my life:

Broken
Confused
Embarrassed
Angry
Discouraged
Fearful
Anxious
Depressed
Desperate
Ashamed
Disappointed.

And the question in the front of my mind, "How did I allow myself to get here, again?"

Well, the answer I uncovered in therapy is primarily because I never allowed little girl Debbie and the young woman Debbie to ever take a moment to comprehend and feel all the emotions in their entirety. I never took the time to just sit in the loss, hurt, fear and abandonment I had experienced so many times. I didn't know I was being tormented. All I knew was that I could not see my way out. But I can say with complete confidence that the phrase that helped me overcome all the tormenting thoughts and broken pieces of my heart was, "If I can live through my mother's death, then I can live through this." And I moved on.

I tucked all my emotions deep inside as was my custom and went back to feeling like "Why did I trust God?" I guess I wasn't ready to look in the mirror. I didn't want to admit that I did see the red flags in my past relationships. And all because I had to have the fantasy, the fairy tale. I had to have the family, the house, the white picket fence, and the kids. But the fantasy was short-lived.

I wanted my big happy family and that last time I thought I had just walked into it. The biggest attraction for me was that this man was in the church. That was huge since I had not seen that with any prior men I dealt with and for my new life in Christ, that was bigger than anything for me. I believed he was living his life for God. He was living the Word, and he loved God the way Christ loves the church. That's how I saw him. What I would not allow myself to see, however, was the controlling personality or OCD and other behaviors he exhibited, because I wanted my dream. I guess I wanted my dream, - my fantasy - more than I wanted to be happy. But in the end, we both were just two halves that came together thinking that we were gonna make a whole. Don't be fooled. It may sound cute but both parties need to be whole just to get off on the right foot.

I was broken and he was broken. So two broken people coming together to make one big broken life created a disaster. And I had to learn, and I say to you, if there is no healing, no deliverance and no one being set free before you marry, then you bring all of those issues into your marriage. He brought his, and I brought mine, and we each were looking for the other to fix what was wrong with us, rather than allowing God to heal us himself.

All of these thoughts were swirling in my head as Greg and I were splitting up because I could see how much my husband was **not** going to be there for me. I looked at this man I had just married and thought, "how could the man I thought would take all my past pains away so easily drop me the way he did." And yes I know I shouldn't have expected a man to do that, that's Jesus. Nonetheless, I questioned "if Jesus had cleansed me and made me whole, why was this happening?" And the only answer I could come up with again was that Jesus was a man too, that's why!

Chapter 9

Broken Woman Syndrome (Who Am I?)

 The secret of change is not to focus all your energy on fighting the old, but on building the new.

~Socrates

So back into the world I went. I would leave Alexandria, Virginia and move to Richmond. I stopped going to church and stopped serving God. All I focused on was work and partying. Yes, partying. My heart was so full of pain that my mind was not thinking rationally. One night while feeling very down and lonely, I went to this lounge in Richmond. I definitely had way too much to drink, and that evening I met a man named Dwayne. He was tall, dark and handsome, smart, and a gentleman. He knew I was in no condition to drive, so he offered to take me home. Of course, I said no because I didn't know him. Fortunately, he was a perfect gentleman and actually followed me home and made sure I was safe.

From that encounter and him making sure I was alright, we started communicating and soon became a couple. I felt so happy. Our families connected, and my friends loved him. My children even loved him. But I had to put my five-year rule in place. If he didn't ask me to marry him within that time, I was gone. Well, he did ask me.

Looking back, I know now that I put too much pressure on the relationship. We each fell deeply in love and of course, in my mind, this was it for real this time. I had what I called my "Etta James moment," from the song made famous by the old soul and blues singer back in 1960, *"At last … my love has come along."* So Dwayne and I got engaged. We reached out to friends and family to be bridesmaids and groomsmen. We were to be married in July 2013. I had already bought my gown, booked the place for our reception, and picked out the bridesmaids' dresses. And the invitations were about to go out.

On January 30, 2013, I slipped and fell on my leg at work. The bone came through my ankle on my right leg, and I had a compound fracture. I had to endure two surgeries. The doctors inserted a plate in my ankle, but my body rejected it and caused an infection. The doctors put me on their strongest bacterial infection medicine drip and had a nurse coming to the house once a week to change my bandages. At one point, the prognosis for my ankle was so bad they didn't know if they would have to amputate my foot.

While enduring the surgeries and recovery, Dwayne and I started growing apart instead of closer as a couple. I could not believe his response to me in all this and started thinking that suffering emotional pain was evidently the life I was chosen to live. When Dwayne was at work, my girls Shona, Claudia, and Louise would come to take care of me. I also thankfully had Devon, Kevin, and Tina to help as well. Devon and Kevin are Dwayne's sister and brother. Tina is his mother. They were all there for me, even Dwayne. It just wasn't the same. I don't know at what point love stopped living in our home. I just know it did. We called off the wedding.

All I can say is, but God!!! The last thing I needed at that point in my life was to be in another failing relationship. I had not even gotten over the wounds from my marriage. I am forever thankful for God's intervention, because I definitely was not in my right mind, no matter how nice and caring this man seemed.

So this human breaking my heart allowed me to see that God does not love like we love. I was learning that God's love supersedes anything and everything that we even think. As a result, we mess up this love thing again and again because we have such a limited and conditional view of love. It's like our love is this box, but God's love is the universe. And in our box are all the irreconcilable differences that we cannot overcome while God is over to the side, not even remembering the sins we committed against him because of his Son's sacrifice. Learning what true love is has helped me to be who I am right now. It has literally allowed me to look at anyone who has ever hurt me and forgive them.

But understand, initially, when I was still new to the things of God, I did forgive, but only because God said we had to. I used to say, "God, I forgive them with my mouth, but in my heart I don't know if I'm really forgiving them because I'm still feeling the pain and the hurt." If I saw that person out somewhere and still felt some type of way, I knew I haven't truly forgiven them then. Yet now my forgiveness is real. It often shocks me that God's love has penetrated my heart so deeply because now I can love past my pain. Even the people at work notice it because they know when someone has said something about me and I can still minister to that person. My close co-workers are like, "Girl, how can you do that?" I would say, "Chile, that is not me. Me in the flesh, the old country girl would have been ready to take him down." But I am no longer that 50% Cardi B and 50% Claire Huxtable, I was walking out my faith 100% Jesus. And it was crazy too, but once God's pure love penetrated my heart, all I could see when someone hurt me was Jesus up on that cross for me, therefore I could easily let it go. I knew what my sins were and the cost Jesus bore for me, so I had grace for others who mess up just like me. I didn't want God to have anything against me he wouldn't let go.

And from that foundation of forgiveness, God's therapy became instrumental in allowing me to identify and heal from all the wounds I had carried for so long.

***

Finally, after getting clarity on all that I had experienced since I was 13 years old, I made one of the best decisions of my new life, to go back to church.

I remember waking up super early one Sunday morning, getting dressed and then leaving to go to my car. I left my apartment complex's parking lot not knowing what church I was going to. I just knew I had to get to a church. I ended up parking at the Faith and Family Church, where Pastor Calvin Duncan and First Lady Barbara Duncan were leading. As I entered, everyone at the church was so loving and welcoming. They made me feel really good walking into the service. As I sat down, one of the members, Laverne, came and sat by me. She just hugged on me and welcomed me to the service.

As Pastor Duncan began to teach, tears started streaming down my face to the point that the hurt was coming through my voice. I remember Laverne taking me and putting me in her arms and consoling me. When I finally got myself together and could lift my head, I found myself lying in the arms of First Lady Barbara. I could not believe it! I didn't even know when the exchange had taken place, but her love for people had moved her from the pulpit to come see about me. Needless to say I rededicated my life to Christ and joined the church.

This church was instrumental in God allowing me to get to the other side of all that had plagued me for so many years. I remember one bible study, when towards the end, Pastor Duncan looked out at me and asked me my name. It was weird since I'm sure he knew, but I said "Debbie." Then he asked again and I told him Debbie again. Yet for some reason, this did not satisfy him and even Pastor Barbara picked up on his question this time and said, "Pastor, you know her name is

'Debbie.'" Then Pastor Duncan said, "Is that the name your mother gave you?" And it was at that moment that I knew something was happening, but I was not sure what. So hesitantly I told him, "Well, when my mother would get angry or really wanted my attention, she would call me "Deborah." And he immediately said "Yes, that's it. That's your name – Deborah," as if he had uncovered some mystery.

But what I would experience in what I now know was a divine encounter would not only be the correct pronunciation of "Deborah," which is "duh-boar-ah" but that there was a great woman in the Bible named Deborah who led Israel to a military victory by freeing them from their captivity by the Canaanites. Deborah was an ordinary woman who, because of her righteousness and courage as a prophetess, was made a judge over all Israel. Her faith, wisdom, fairness, and obedience to the Lord was widely regarded. She had been deeply concerned over the ill-treatment of her people who were suffering at the hands of their Canaanite enemies (Judges 4 and 5). Pastor Duncan felt this calling on my life. This became another point of growth as God started to remove the shackles off of my life. After that encounter, I started calling myself by my God-given name, and so does everyone else now - Deborah!

In fact, this new season was my pivot from God. This was the final session of therapy I needed. And as I continued to grow in knowledge and faith, which I knew was to be an ongoing journey, God had me transferred to another store location in Charlottesville, Virginia. However my church continued to be Faith and Family Church where I am still planted.

Gaining Strength
(Lessons Learned)

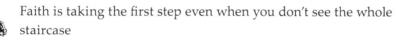

Faith is taking the first step even when you don't see the whole staircase

~Dr. Martin Luther King, Jr.

When I finally stopped running, I was able to face the brokenness in my life.

What about you?

Have you ever been so tired that you didn't know what to do? That when you looked over your life you saw nothing but the traumas that have plagued you and caused fear to take up residency in your heart?

Have you pushed yourself so hard and for so long that you don't even know how to just be, just be at peace. That even when there's nothing wrong, you're still waiting for the bottom to fall out.

In my perspective, no matter what good thing I was doing, I didn't have a sense of peace. No matter what I accomplished, I still didn't feel good enough. When I set out to get my bachelor's degree while working my full-time job as a store manager, which required me to travel, I jumped at the opportunity. In this role, I could run away from my inner disappointments, trauma, and turmoil. It took me seven years, but I did it. I got that bachelor's degree in human services.

However, in my mind, I was still not good enough. It did not matter that I was working, and even leading a team. I was not only a store manager, but I oversaw several different stores. In fact, I achieved the highest honor you can get in retail, the President's Club Award . But still, I did not feel good enough. I needed more validation. I went back to school to get my master's degree. Yet, even after completing my MBA, my eyes still couldn't see me the way God sees me. I couldn't see myself through His eyes. I needed more.

I would later enroll in a health and life coaching class from the Health Coach Institute. I completed that program and became a Certified Health and Life Coach. I had accomplished so many external things, but tell me, why was I still crying myself to sleep at night? One very long night as I cried out, God so gently showed me the little girl inside of me that I would not let die.

This was the little girl that never had a chance to be a little girl. The little girl who needed to express her hurts, her pains, and her disappointments. But how could she when ...

- My family depended on me to be strong.
- My friends depended on me to be strong.
- My team depended on me to be strong.
- My children, especially, depended on me to be strong,
- My daughter even has me listed as Superwoman in her phone.

That little girl inside me was there, but she had been buried so deep that she was suffocating. She needed air. She needed light. She needed for the cry of her heart to be heard, so she could be healed and delivered.

And that's who I saw when I looked in the mirror. No matter how big I had gotten, or how fancy my clothes, makeup, or jewelry were, when I saw myself, that's who I saw; a lost little girl, a fraud even, I thought.

I couldn't even celebrate my accomplishments.

I must not be good enough I thought, since my own dad didn't want me.

I can't even keep a relationship; I've been married and divorced, twice.

These were the thoughts that continually invaded my mind. So I continued to work and stay busy so that I didn't have time to think or remember all the broken pieces of my heart. I was trying to forget and not resurrect that dead little girl inside of me. But God was coming for me.

He would not let me go. It got to the point where I felt like the scene in the Bible when Jesus put the people out of the house and went into the room and called to the little girl, *"Talitha koum!... Little girl I need for you to arise."* Mark 5:40-41.

And rise she did.

God started putting new thoughts in her mind. He taught her how to focus on his Word and what He said, and to reject any thought that did not sound like him, a loving Father. He taught her what true love is.

And that little girl started to believe it.

She started to remember he had always been there with her. That His word said that He would never leave us nor forsake us.

And He hadn't.

He was there all the time.

So she got up.

She rose with power, knowing how much she was loved by her Heavenly Father.

And it was only in that revelation that she finally found what she had been looking for all her life. She had been desperate, desperate to be seen, so desperate for the father she never knew and the one who was burdened with his own battles, to love her. But they could not give her what they themselves did not have. They only knew conditional love. They only knew love that just lasted through the night, or for a moment. But that wasn't enough. She needed the kind of love that lasts, that remains, that will come running after you to rescue you from all the fears and hurts and pains and bring you into peace. That's what she needed.

And finally, that's what she received.

How about you? Wouldn't you like to receive this as well?

I know you do and I pray that the words in this work bring you peace, encouragement, deliverance, and most of all, healing for those broken places in your heart. It's time to take your heart back. Proverbs 4:23 says, *"above all else, guard your heart, for everything you do flows from it."*

Another gem God gave me was to think back to who I was before the pain. When did I make the decision that suffering emotional pain was the life I was chosen to live. And in finding those answers, I had to ask, *Who am I now?* I was so weighted with shame, guilt, depression and other ills that I had neglected to celebrate what I did know, what I had accomplished and who I had become in the midst of pain. This lesson I learned from my coach. One time he asked me who I am. I answered I'm a store manager. I have a health and life coaching certificate. I do some life coaching, and I have a Master's degree in business administration because I'm going to be my own CEO. Then he stopped me. Just completely stopped me and said, "I didn't ask what you do, I asked who you are?"

Honestly, it took me a minute as I could not answer him at that moment. I left the meeting struggling within myself trying to respond to that question. I remember sitting on the corner of my bed looking at myself in the mirror and wondering who am I? As tears rolled down my face I prayed and asked God to show me, me. I don't recall how long I sat there staring at myself in silence, but I remember the Holy Spirit ever so gently speaking to my spirit that I am who God says I am.

I am royalty.
I am chosen.
I am the apple of God's eye.
I am loved.
I am favored.
I am more than a conqueror.
I am beautifully and wonderfully made in His image.

And I smiled. I smiled because that was surely not the soundtrack that had been playing in my head for so many years. God reminded me that although it wasn't normal for me to go through everything that I've been through, He was celebrating me because my heart still desired to serve Him. That my heart was full of love and forgiveness. That my heart longs to bring value to other people. A heart that desires to help people turn their pain into power and purpose.

God was teaching me to call on the inner strength that was already within me to fight. He told me he has already given me courage and good character. He told me to be resilient, because He himself was protecting me, providing for me and keeping me. He told me not to fear. That His unfailing, unconditional love would sustain me. And in that moment, His peace washed over me with such a power that

I was transformed. I have never felt so loved in all of my life. God loves me. God loves me. He absolutely, unequivocally loves me. And He loves you too.

Conclusion

The Lioness Emerges (The Real Me)

> "The strength of a woman is not measured by the impact that all her hardships in life have had on her, but the strength of a woman is measured by the extent of her refusal to allow hardships to dictate her and so she becomes."
>
> ~C Joy Bell C.

I call myself the Lioness because this is who I now see when I look in the mirror. My definition of the Lioness is that of *A Mother, a Female, or a Queen. The Lioness is a magnificent image of strength, passion, and beauty. She stands as a fierce defender of her family and a more than capable provider. In groups, the lionesses become a creative and strategic force to be reckoned with, acting as one to change the world around them.*

God has been calling me to a greater, more excellent place for decades. And by greater, I mean He has told me that there are some things and people he wants me to impact. My life is worth it, and His plans for me are good.

But I had no understanding of this. For most of my life, from childhood, I have been suffering in silence. The suffering started as anxiety when I saw my mother constantly being abused. It then turned into depression as I functioned in a never-ending role of responsibility to care about and for others, as first, my mother died, then Granny. I had no option but to be responsible, but I never really got a chance to be the girl whose soul needed to grieve the loss of her two most important relationships.

And what others saw was only a facade. The average person observing my confidence level on the outside in the face of what we were experiencing thought I was handling my business. But on the inside, I was going through turmoil, and nobody knew but God and me.

I spent many years asking God questions like:

Why was I so depressed?
Why did I feel rejected so much?
Why did I feel abandoned?
Why wasn't I good enough?
Why can I get beyond my past?
Why am I so afraid to do what you called me to do?

The questions left me feeling like I was an imposter. Especially when it came to doing what God wanted me to do. Remember, I still saw myself as that shy girl from Filbert, Pennsylvania. "*Who is going to listen to me?*" I thought, doubting my abilities and feeling like a fraud. When God told me to write my story, I responded, "*I can't write a book, and I can't be a transformational coach, either.*" So the dream continued to lie dormant in me for decades. And over those years, this small knowing was inside me that I was created for something much greater. It would not go away, and God would not let me rest.

And like Moses in the Bible, at one point, he also felt inadequate because he stuttered. He committed murder when he saw someone mistreated, thinking he was in the right until he was found out. Then he questioned everything about himself when God called him to use that anger to bring his people out of bondage. I believe Moses, too, asked God, "I'm sure you know my past. I'm not even who I thought I was. Why would you give me this assignment?

I saw myself in these similarities: the stuttering, the shyness, and the impostor syndrome, which he had. Recall how he questioned why God would want him to lead his people after he had to run away after killing the Egyptian. This is the same Moses who, as a baby, was rescued from the Nile River, raised in the Pharaoh's palace, and instructed in the knowledge and training of the greatest kingdom at that time. Yet, he wondered, "who am I?" But God told him, "I Am that I Am," and I Am Sovereign. That means I can do whatever I want. I can have you in the halls of Egypt or on the backside of the mountain because I Am God. I know the plans I have for your life. Plans to prosper you, not to harm you, and give you hope and a future. (Jeremiah 29:11)

And this is now who I am. God's lioness. The one He called before I was even formed in my mother's womb, and who knew every trial I would encounter. And what I have learned through it all is that He is my fairy tale, The One I had been seeking all along. It's funny how we have to go through so much to get to what we've had all along. But now I see with His eyes and what I see is beautiful. I Am Beautiful. Beautifully Broken.

Thank you, Mom

I hope I have made you proud!

About Deborah Blakey

Deborah Blakey is a Transformational Heart-Healing Coach, entrepreneur, leader, businesswoman, sister, mother, mentor, friend, grandmother, and author. She is originally from Brownsville, PA, and has spent much of her life in Virginia. Deborah has multiple degrees and certifications, including a Master's in Business Administration, Health and Life Coach certification from the Health Coach Institute, and a Transformational Coaching Certification under Dr. Dharius Daniels.

A defining scripture that brings her life is Romans 8:38-39: "For I am convinced that neither death nor life, neither angels nor demons, neither the present nor the future, nor any powers, neither height nor depth, nor anything else in all creation, will be able to separate us from the love of God that is in Christ Jesus our Lord."

Deborah is best known for bringing out the best version in everyone and adding unforgettable value to the lives of each person that she encounters. Her mission is to help others live free by promoting self-love, belief, and value through overcoming crises of the heart. As a Transformational Heart-Healing Coach, she helps people dealing with emotional problems connect with their souls, find clarity, and discover their voice. Deborah is a teacher and coach and a model of "practice what you preach."

As stated in Proverbs 4:23, she emphasizes guarding the heart above all else, as this is the source from which everything flows and determines the course of life. She walks and lives as an example of God's love, turning trials into triumphs. This resolute woman of God decided to dedicate her life to God and follow her true passion, calling, and purpose by adopting the affirmation "I. Am. Life." This represented the pivotal point in her life when she began to live the life she loved instead of just existing. The transformation, the beautiful brokenness, the journey to self-love, discovering a new outlook on life and pouring into others, and now, pouring into you. Deborah Blakey is a Lioness.

You can reach her at www.thelionnesswithin.com.

Made in the USA
Middletown, DE
07 March 2023

26289691R00053